STORIES FROM WORLD RELIGIONS

STORIES FROM WORLD RELIGIONS

Retold by Anita Ganeri

Illustrated by Jackie Morris

HODDER

Wayland

an imprint of Hodder Children's Books

To Anna, Tom and Matthew – AG
For James and Mari Mayhew – JM

First published in hardback under the title 'Journeys through Dreamtime' in 1998
by Macdonald Young Books, an imprint of Wayland Publishers Ltd
This paperback edition published in 2005
by Hodder Wayland, an imprint of Hodder Children's Books

Text © Anita Ganeri 1998
Illustrations © Jackie Morris 1998

Commissioning editor: Hazel Songhurst
Designer: Kate Buxton

Printed and bound in China
ISBN 07502 4737 1

Hodder Children's Books
a division of Hodder Headline Limited,
338 Euston Road London, NW1 3BH

CONTENTS

INTRODUCTION Page 7

INTRODUCTION

The stories in this collection come from some of the world's great religions and faiths. Most of these are still practised today, by millions of people all over the world. Many of the tales are very ancient, first told hundreds or even thousands of years ago, by storytellers or religious teachers and leaders. The stories were often used to explain their teachings, preach a difficult message or moral, or to explain the world around them. In the ancient world, storytelling was an important way of passing on knowledge, history, news and views. Storytellers needed excellent memories – many of the stories in this book were at first learned off by heart, then passed on by word of mouth. They were not written down in book form until hundreds of years later.

In this book, the stories have been divided into sections, each based around its own topic or theme. There are tales of gods, goddesses and heroes, and stories of saints, angels and immortals. Some stories tell of the holiest places in various religions and of the journeys devout followers make to visit them. There are stories explaining why certain feasts and festivals are celebrated as holy days, and still others describing how the natural wonders of the world came to be, at a time when people did not know enough to understand them scientifically.

Whatever their message or theme, these are stories designed to stir your thoughts and your imagination. Wherever you come from, and wherever you may be going, treasure their magic and enjoy this journey through dreamtime.

THE FIRST MAN AND THE GODDESS

This story from Africa tells how the first man set out to win the hand of a beautiful goddess in marriage.

Long ago in Africa lived Kintu, the first man on Earth. He was all alone apart from a cow who gave him fine fresh milk to drink. One day the goddess Nambi, daughter of the god of the Sky, came down to Earth. She fell deeply in love with Kintu but her father, Gulu, would not allow them to marry. First, he wanted to set Kintu five difficult tests to prove he would make a worthy husband.

For the first test, Gulu stole Kintu's cow and hid it in Heaven. With no milk to drink, Kintu was forced to live on leaves and nearly starved. But Nambi knew what had happened and told Kintu to go to Heaven and bring back the cow. As soon as Kintu reached Heaven, however, Gulu set him another test. Instead of starving poor Kintu this time, he locked him in a hut with enough food to feed a hundred people.

'If you can't eat it all, you'll be killed,' he told him.

Kintu ate and ate as much as he could, until he could eat no more. Then he hid the rest in a hole he made in the floor and showed Gulu the empty plates. Gulu was sure Kintu had tricked him.

'I'll show him,' he thought.

For the third test he gave Kintu a copper axe and ordered him to chop up rocks as small as firewood.

The task seemed hopeless. But Kintu found a large chunk of rock, already quite splintered and cracked, and he managed to break off some slivers.

Gulu was furious. He didn't like to be outdone.

He gave Kintu a large water pot and told him to fill it with dew. Kintu put the pot on the ground while he thought what to do. Where on Earth would he find enough dew? But, lo and behold, when he picked the pot up again, he found it brim full with dew.

By now, even Gulu was impressed by Kintu's cleverness.

'You have my blessing for your marriage,' he told Kintu. 'If you complete the last test. Go and fetch your cow. It is in the field with my own herds of cattle.'

But when Kintu reached the field he saw how cunning Gulu had been. For all the cows in the field looked exactly the same, all exactly like his own cow.

'I'll never marry Nambi now,' he groaned. 'It's hopeless.'

Just then, a bumblebee flew by and hovered right by Kintu's ear.

'Don't despair,' it buzzed. 'Wait until evening and pick the cow whose horns I land on.'

That evening, Kintu watched closely as the cowherd drove the cows down the field ready for milking. As the first herd passed by, the bumblebee stayed in a nearby tree so Kintu knew that none of these cows was his. The same thing happened with the second herd. But when the third herd appeared, the bee flew off and landed on the horns of Kintu's long-lost cow. Then, to his great delight and pleasure, the bee buzzed away again and landed on the horns of three new calves. They had been born while the cow was in Gulu's Heaven.

So, Kintu passed his tests with flying colours and he and Nambi were married amid great rejoicing. Soon after the wedding they set off back to Earth. They took with them the cow and her calves, a sheep, a goat, a hen, a yam and a banana – all the things that people on Earth needed to live happily ever after.

THE DAY THE SUN
HID HER FACE

The Japanese god of the seas, Susanowo, was famous for his terrible temper.
One day, he quarrelled with his sister, the goddess of the Sun, Amaterasu,
and plunged the whole world into darkness.

In the Shinto religion of Japan, there is a story which tells of the
fateful day when the Sun went out and the Earth was plunged into
darkness. The great goddess, Amaterasu, was the goddess of the Sun.
Her brother, Susanowo, was lord of the seas. But whereas his sister
was gentle and kind, Susanowo had a terrible temper. He ranted and raged and
neglected his duties. Nothing was ever his own fault. One day, his father could stand
it no longer. He banished his son to the Land of Darkness, deep, deep beneath the
Earth. Before he left, Susanowo asked a favour:

'Father, I wish to visit my sister in Heaven,' he said, 'and bid her farewell.'

To keep the peace, his father agreed.

Amaterasu was busy in the sacred weaving hall where she and her maids made
clothes for the gods. When news reached her that her brother was coming,
she feared the worst. She armed herself with a bow and arrows
and prepared for battle.

'I haven't come to cause any trouble,' Susanowo told her. 'I just wanted to say goodbye to you.'

'I do not believe you,' the goddess replied. 'Prove that you are telling the truth!'

They agreed to hold a contest. If Susanowo could beat his sister into producing five strong sons, Amaterasu would believe him. The contest began. Amaterasu took her brother's sword and gave him her necklace in return. These they washed in the Well of Heaven. Then Amaterasu broke the sword into pieces and Susanowo smashed the beads from her necklace. Then together they blew out a long, long breath of air. From the Sun goddess's breath came three beautiful daughters. From her brother's breath came. . . five strong sons.

While Susanowo celebrated his victory by conjuring up a terrible storm, Amaterasu stayed silent. Finally, she spoke:

'The victory is mine,' she announced. 'For your sons came from my necklace.'

'Nonsense!' howled Susanowo.

'You're just a bad loser!' he screamed.

'I'll show you!' he raged. And he picked up his horse and hurled it through the roof of the hall.

Amaterasu was terrified. She had never seen her brother so angry before. Before matters could get worse, she ran away and hid in a deep, dark cave.

And this is how the Sun went out and Heaven and Earth grew dark and cold. In despair, the eight hundred gods of Heaven met in council by the Sacred River. Whatever should they do? How could they coax Amaterasu to come out of her cave?

The wisest god, Omirokane, was given the task of finding the answer. For days he sat deep in thought until the other gods grew impatient. At last, he told one god to make a magic rope of jewels and another to make a magic mirror. The rope and the mirror were hung from the branches of a sacred tree which the gods had planted outside the cave. Then the goddess of the dawn climbed on to an upturned tub and began to dance. She hopped first on one leg, then on the other, she jumped in the air and whirled round and round. Suddenly, she fell off the tub and landed in a heap on the ground. The eight hundred gods laughed so much that the ground shook as if it had been hit by an earthquake.

Inside her cave, Amaterasu heard the noise and wondered what was happening. She peeped outside.

'Why are you making so much noise?' she asked the goddess.

'We're celebrating,' the goddess replied. 'We've found a goddess even greater than you. Come and see.'

Two of the gods held up the magic mirror and the god of strength hid nearby. Slowly, Amaterasu crept out of the cave. But where was this goddess? All she could see was her own reflection in a mirror. Just then, the god of strength grabbed her hand and pulled her out into the open. Quick as a flash, the other gods stretched the magic jewel rope across the cave mouth to stop her going back inside.

So, Amaterasu returned to the world and the Sun returned to the sky. The rice fields bloomed and people rejoiced. One by one, the gods came forward and bowed before the goddess, begging her never to hide her shining face again.

As for Susanowo, he was finally banished to the Land of Darkness, never to return to Heaven again. And this was the harshest punishment there could be.

THE GREAT HERO'S BIRTH

In the Jain religion of India, a man called Mahavira is the great hero, the last and greatest of twenty-four teachers who appeared on Earth to save the world. Many legends surround Mahavira's birth and life.

From his home in Heaven, Mahavira chose the wife of an Indian king, Queen Trishala, to be his earthly mother. Before he was born, his mother dreamt that her son would be great. In one dream she saw a huge white elephant with four gleaming tusks of purest gold. In other dreams she saw a noble bull and a lion, the Moon and the Sun, a lotus pond and an ocean of milk. These were all signs that her son would be a hero. On the night Mahavira was born, the Earth shook in honour and the whole world was in awe. The gods and goddesses descended from Heaven to pay their respects to the world's new saviour. Even mighty Indra, king of the gods, bowed down before him.

While his earthly parents were alive, Mahavira lived happily with them. He married a princess, Yashodara, and had a beautiful daughter. But when his parents died, Mahavira left the comfort of his home and family and set off to find the meaning of life. Once again the gods came to honour him. They carried him in a golden carriage to a leafy forest where, wearing only a simple white robe, he sat under a tree in deep meditation. And as Mahavira sat and meditated, the truth he was seeking became clear to him. He taught what he learned first to the gods, then to the people and many of them became his disciples. When he was 73 years old, Mahavira died. He returned to his home in the highest Heaven where, bathed in light, he sits on a shining diamond throne.

DAVID AND GOLIATH

This story is told in the Hebrew (Jewish) Bible and in the Old Testament
of the Christian Bible. It tells of how, against the odds, the hero, David,
killed the giant, Goliath.

In the reign of King Saul of Israel, a great battle took place between
the Israelites and their enemies the Philistines. On the eve of the
battle, the Israelites gathered on one side of a valley; on the other
stood the Philistines. Suddenly a gigantic man appeared from among
the Philistines' ranks. He was the mighty Goliath, more than three metres tall and
the strongest fighter in the world. He wore a brass helmet on his head and heavy
chain mail on his body. Holding a huge iron spear in one hand, he stepped forward
and challenged the Israelites.

'Send one of your soldiers to fight me,' he boomed, in a voice which spread fear
through their ranks. 'If he kills me, you will have won and we Philistines will
become your servants. But if I kill him, you must serve us.'

The Israelites were terrified. They did not know what to do. For forty days they
talked and talked but could not agree on a solution. And every day, morning and
night, Goliath stood up and repeated his challenge.

Far away from the battle ground, a shepherd boy was tending his father's sheep.
His name was David, and his three eldest brothers were serving in the Israelite
army. One day Jesse, his father, said to him:

'David, I have an errand for you. Take this bread and cheese to your brothers
tomorrow and see what news there is.'

Early next morning, David set off. He arrived just as battle was about to begin.
As he searched for his brothers a hush fell on the army, for the giant Goliath stood
before them again booming out his challenge.

'The King has sworn to reward the person who kills Goliath with great wealth
and his daughter's hand in marriage,' said one of the soldiers to David.

When David's brother saw him talking to the soldiers they were angry
and told him to go home. But King Saul summoned David and was
astonished by what he had to say.

'I will fight the giant, Goliath,' said David, bravely. 'God will watch over me and protect me from harm.'

Saul tried to persuade David to change his mind.

'You are just a young boy,' he said, gently. 'And Goliath has been a fighter all his life. How can you beat him?'

But David repeated that he was not afraid. So Saul gave him his own mail coat and helmet and fastened on his own sword. But David could not walk in the heavy armour and took it off. Instead, he took his wooden staff in his hand and chose five smooth stones from a nearby brook. Then he picked up his sling and walked over to face Goliath. When the giant saw David, he laughed loudly and long.

'What is this I see?' he scoffed and sneered. 'A boy? Go home, boy, and look after your sheep. Before I really lose my temper.'

David looked calmly at the giant. He pulled a stone from his bag and put it in his sling. Then, quick as a flash, he hurled it with all his might straight at Goliath's head.

The stone sped through the air and hit Goliath so hard that it sunk deep into his forehead. For a moment he tottered and swayed on his feet. Then he staggered and fell to the ground with an enormous thud.

And so, David the shepherd boy killed Goliath the mighty champion. The Israelites shouted and cheered, while the terrified Philistines turned tail and fled. Amid great celebration, Saul took David back to his palace where he married his daughter, Michal. And when Saul died, David became King of Israel in his place and ruled justly and fairly for forty years.

THE TEN LIVES OF VISHNU

In the Hindu religion, people worship hundreds of different gods and goddesses.
The three greatest gods are Brahma, the creator of the universe,
Vishnu, the protector, and Shiva, the destroyer of evil.

The great Hindu god, Vishnu, is worshipped as the protector of the Universe. He has appeared on Earth ten times in different guises. Each time, he comes to save the world and its people from danger. These ten appearances are called avatars. In between times, Vishnu sleeps in the Ocean of Heaven, lying on the coils of the great Serpent of Eternity.

The first avatar was the fish, Matsya. He saved the world from a terrible flood.

The second was Kurma, a tortoise. He helped to churn the ocean of milk and win back the gods' lost elixir of life.

The third avatar was Varaha, a boar as big as a mountain. He rescued the Earth from the demons who had dragged it down into their watery den.

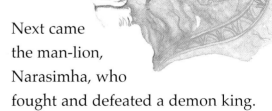

Next came the man-lion, Narasimha, who fought and defeated a demon king.

Vishnu's fifth avatar was the dwarf, Vamana. He defeated a demon who tried to push Indra, king of the gods, out of Heaven.

The sixth avatar was Parasurama, the warrior who destroyed the thousand-armed king of the mountains.

The seventh avatar was the hero, Rama, whose story is told in a famous poem, the Ramayana. With the help of the monkey-god, Hanuman, he rescued Sita, his wife, who had been kidnapped by Ravana, evil king of Lanka.

Vishnu's eighth avatar was the blue god, Krishna. You can read about him on the next page.

Ninth came the Buddha, the founder of the Buddhist faith.

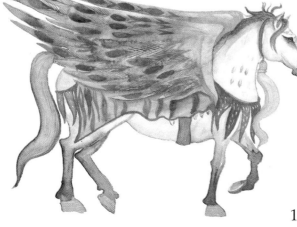

Vishnu's tenth and last avatar is yet to come. This will be Kalki, a great white horse, sent to get rid of all sin and wickedness.

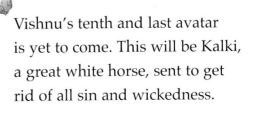

HOW KRISHNA SAVED THE RIVER

There are many stories about Krishna, the blue god, who was Vishnu's eighth avatar.
In this tale, he saves his village from an evil serpent.

 When Krishna was born his life was in danger. His wicked uncle, King Kamsa, had vowed to kill him. He was afraid that one day Krishna would seize his throne. So one dark night, Krishna's father crept out of the palace and took his baby son to the house of Nanda, a cowherd. Nanda and his wife lived by the banks of the Yamuna River. They loved and cared for Krishna and kept him safe from his uncle's fury. Krishna grew up to be very fond of mischief and often played tricks on his friends. But he was also the god Vishnu in one of his guises, and he performed many great deeds as well.

One fine summer's day, Krishna and his friends the cowherds were wandering along the banks of the river with their cows. The day was hot and they were thirsty so they stopped by the water to drink. But as soon as the water touched the lips of the cows and cowherds they fell down dead on the ground. For a terrible five-headed serpent, the monstrous Kaliya, had come to live in the river and the water had soon been filled with the lethal poison that oozed from his five sets of fangs. With a touch and a glance, Krishna revived his companions.

'Whatever happened?' they asked as they woke up.

When Krishna told them, they were filled with despair.

'But what shall we do?' they groaned. 'Without the river, we'll have nothing to drink. And no water for the cows.'

'Don't worry,' said Krishna. 'I will save you.'

So Krishna went down the river and found its deepest, darkest pool. For this is where Kaliya had made his home. The water boiled and hissed with Kaliya's poison and gave off deadly fumes. Birds fell down dead as they flew overhead and all the fish that once lived there had died. The dreadful serpent himself was nowhere to be seen, but Krishna knew that he was waiting. He climbed to the top of a very tall tree, clapped his hands and dived into the water.

As Krishna swam across the pool, Kaliya slithered menacingly out of his den. Furious at being disturbed, he caught the blue god in his mighty coils – coils so strong they could crush you to death. And then he began to squeeze. For a while Krishna stayed quite still, then, when the serpent relaxed his grip just for a second, he struggled free and jumped on top of his hooded heads. Then Krishna began to dance. He danced on one head, then on another, stamping his feet and kicking and jumping. Kaliya hissed angrily but his strength was soon gone. His heads were crushed under Krishna's feet with a pain that felt like pounding hammers.

Then all of a sudden Krishna stopped. Kaliya gasped for breath and shook himself to ease his aching heads. But the evil serpent had learned his lesson. He bowed his five heads before Krishna and begged the blue god for mercy.

'I will spare you,' said Krishna, 'on one condition. That you leave this river to the cows and cowherds and never return. You must go now to the ocean, far away from here.'

The serpent was only too glad to agree. He turned and swam away down the river on his long journey to the sea. And the river at once became clear and pure for the cows and cowherds to drink.

TOBIAS AND THE ANGEL

This Christian story comes from the Apocrypha,
found between the Old and New Testaments in some editions of the Bible.

There was once a man called Tobit who lived in the land of Nineveh. Tobit was well known for his acts of kindness and for his charity. He shared his food with the hungry and gave away his clothes to the poor. For many years, Tobit was content with his life. But one terrible day, an accident left him blind and made him feel that his life was worthless. In despair, he prayed to God and asked him to save him from his dreadful misery.

Meanwhile, in the land of Media, a young woman was also praying for God's help. Her name was Sarah and her father, Raguel, was Tobit's cousin. Sarah had been taken over by a wicked demon who killed any man who wanted to marry her. She despaired of ever finding a husband and prayed to God to get rid of the demon.

And, high in Heaven, God heard their prayers and sent his angel Raphael down to Earth to help them.

One day, Tobit called his beloved son Tobias to him.

'My son,' he said. 'Go to Media and bring back the silver I left with my cousin, Raguel. I cannot work now I am blind and we must have money to live on.'

'But Father,' Tobias said. 'How will I find the way?' Before Tobit could answer there was a knock at the door. It was a young man, asking for work.

'Have you ever been to Media?' Tobias asked the stranger.

'Many times,' he replied. 'I know the way well.'

So Tobias hired the young man to be his guide to Media. He had no idea that the stranger was the angel Raphael in disguise.

Tobias and the angel set off early next morning. They travelled all day before pitching their camp by the side of a river. As Tobias went to bathe, a huge fish leapt out of the water and tried to swallow him up.

'Catch the fish!' cried the angel. 'We can eat its flesh and use its heart and gall as medicine. The heart is good for getting rid of demons; the gall for curing blindness.'

Tobias did as he was told. They ate the fish and cut out its heart and gall bladder.

Next day, they reached Media and knocked on the door of Raguel's house.

'You should ask Raguel's daughter to marry you,' the angel advised Tobias. 'She is looking for a husband and you need a wife.'

'But I have heard she has a demon inside her who kills anyone who asks for her hand,' said Tobias.

'You must use the fish heart,' the angel replied. 'Put it on the fire in your wedding chamber. Its smell will soon frighten the demon away.'

When Tobias saw Sarah, he fell deeply in love with her and asked Raguel for her hand in marriage.

The two were married the very next day. Just in case, Sarah's father had ordered a grave to be dug for Tobias. He was sure that he would be killed by the demon, like the seven others before him. But that night, Tobias burned the fish heart as the angel had told him. Sure enough the terrified demon took flight, never to return.

Next morning, Raguel was overjoyed to see Tobias alive and well. He ordered a great wedding feast to be held. Tobias was the happiest man alive, but was beginning to feel anxious about his father.

'We must take the silver and go back home,' he told Raphael. 'If I don't go home soon, my father will think I am dead.'

A few days later, Tobias set off with Sarah by his side. His father-in-law showered him with gifts of sheep and cattle, camels and donkeys, money, clothes and furniture. The only thing that made Tobias feel sad was his father's lost sight.

'Don't worry,' Raphael, the angel, said. 'Smear your father's eyes with the fish gall and he will see again, I promise you.'

And so it turned out. When Tobias reached home, he smeared his father's eyes with the fish gall and soon his sight was as good as new.

'I can see you, my son, the light of my eyes!' he cried, with joy. 'And your wife, my new daughter! Praise be to God, and to all his holy angels.'

Now there was just one task left: to pay the man who had guided and helped them all in so many ways. They decided to give Raphael half of Tobit's silver.

'Take it, my friend,' said Tobias. 'With thanks for everything you have done.'

'I don't want your money,' said the stranger, smiling. 'All I ask is for you to praise God and do good works in his name. That is worth far more than silver.'

Then a bright shining light surrounded the man, and Tobias and his father knelt down on the ground.

'For I am the angel Raphael,' said the angel. 'Sent from God to answer your prayers. Sarah's demon has fled and Tobit's blindness is cured. My work is done. Now I must leave you.'

And before their astonished eyes, the angel Raphael rose up into Heaven.

FOZAIL, THE ROBBER SAINT

This Muslim story tells how a robber changed his wicked ways to become a saint.

 Once there lived a man called Al-Fozail ibn Iyaz, known as Fozail for short. Fozail was a holy man, a devout Muslim who prayed every day. But, along with his holiness he was also a highwayman. His thieving and stealing were famous far and wide.

Fozail lived in the middle of the desert with his band of villains. He dressed like a holy man in a robe of rough cloth, wore a woollen cap on his head and hung prayer beads around his neck. Night and day, Fozail's gang robbed innocent travellers and pillaged towns and villages. All booty was brought back to Fozail who divided it up among the gang, keeping the best for himself. Anyone who tried to cheat Fozail and keep more than his share was quickly expelled from the gang.

One day, Fozail's men were lying in wait for a rich merchant caravan. One of the merchants had heard rumours of highwaymen in the area. He decided to take action to save some of his gold.

'Even if they take everything else,' he thought. 'I'll have saved this much.'

He left the caravan and spied Fozail's tent by the side of the road. He saw Fozail close by, dressed in his simple robes. The merchant decided to give him his bag of gold for safe-keeping. Surely a holy man would not be a cheat?

'Leave it over there,' said Fozail, pointing to a corner.
'It'll be quite safe, I can guarantee.'

The merchant did as he was told and then went back to the
caravan, only to find it had already been pillaged. All the luggage
had been carried off and his fellow travellers had been gagged and
tied up with ropes.

The merchant set them free, then went back to Fozail to recover
his gold. When he saw Fozail sitting with the robbers and dividing
the spoils, his heart sank into his shoes. Had he given his
gold to a thief? But Fozail called him over.

'Your gold is where you left it,' he said.

'Take it and then go.'

'What did you do that for?' his companions cried angrily.

'I'll tell you why,' Fozail replied. 'That man had faith in me which I repaid by giving him back his gold. Just as I have faith in Allah that he will reward me by forgiving me for my sins. After all, one good turn deserves another.'

Some days later, another caravan passed by. The sound of a man's voice came from it, chanting a verse from the Muslim holiest book, the Qur'an.

'Is it not time for believers to remember Allah with all their hearts?' were the words which reached the ears of Fozail the highwayman. And they had a dramatic effect on him. Fozail was filled with deep remorse and vowed to change his wicked ways. From this day on there would be no more looting and no more pillaging. From this day on the merchants would be safe. But how could he ever make amends for all the damage he had already done?

'I'll beg forgiveness from those I have wronged,' he wept.

All that day he begged forgiveness, and all of the following day. There was only one merchant who would not forgive him easily.

'I'll teach this robber a lesson,' the merchant vowed. 'One he won't forget.'

He pointed to a huge pile of sand and ordered Fozail to move it. Day after day, Fozail shovelled the sand but the pile never grew any smaller. Then one morning, when Fozail was utterly exhausted, a breeze sprang up and blew the sand clean away. The merchant was astonished, but Fozail knew that it was Allah's mercy.

'I have vowed,' said the merchant, 'Not to forgive you until you repay some of my money. Go into my house, and feel under the rug. There you will find a fistful of gold. Bring it to me and I will forgive you.'

The merchant chuckled as Fozail went inside. For there was nothing under the rug but a fistful of soil. But when Fozail felt beneath the rug he brought out a gleaming fistful of gold! At this, the merchant not only forgave Fozail but decided to became a Muslim.

Finally, Fozail asked his wife to forgive him for she had suffered more than anyone. Then, guided by Allah, they set off for the holy city of Makkah. Fozail and his wife settled there and lived in strict simplicity. Soon the fame of Fozail's teaching spread far and wide. From all around, crowds gathered to hear him preach and to seek his blessing and advice. Fozail the robber had become Fozail the saint.

THE GOLDEN APPLES OF IMMORTALITY

The Norsemen, or Vikings, believed that their gods lived for ever, thanks to the golden apples of youth. This is the story of one terrible day when these precious apples were stolen...

 One day three gods were hunting on Earth. They were Odin the king of the gods, Honir the warrior god and Loki the god of mischief and trickery. It had been a long, tiring day and the three gods were famished. They lit a fire to roast an ox, but the meat would not cook. Suddenly, an eagle called to them from a nearby tree.

'I will lift the spell and let your meat roast, if you let me eat my fill first,' it squawked. The gods were too hungry to disagree. But they were greatly dismayed when the eagle swooped down and snatched up all the best meat for itself. All that was left were the bones and scraps. Loki was furious. He picked up a stick and began to beat the eagle as hard as he could. But the eagle was even more cunning than Loki. He grabbed the stick and flew away, dragging Loki across the ground. Desperately, Loki tried to let go of the stick but it was stuck fast to his hands by magic. He was dragged through thorn bushes, across sharp rocks and over icy glaciers until he could bear it no longer.

Battered and bruised, Loki begged the eagle for mercy.

'I'll do anything you want,' he said. 'If only you'll let me go.'

'Very well,' replied the eagle. 'This is your task. Bring me the goddess Idunn and the golden apples of immortality in her care. You have seven days.'

Loki set off at once for Asgard, the home of the gods. How would he persuade Idunn to leave? He knew that she guarded the golden apples with her life. Loki thought long and hard, and at last came up with a cunning trick. He told Idunn that he had seen a tree on Earth laden with golden apples. They were bigger and more beautiful that those she watched over in Asgard.

'I'll show you if you like,' he told her. 'But bring your own apples to compare.' As soon as Idunn set foot on Earth, the eagle swooped down and grabbed her. He carried her at once to the Land of the Giants, for he was really a giant, called Thiazi. It was not long before word of this disaster reached the gods. Without the apples of immortality, they began to grow old and frail. Eventually they would die. They summoned Loki back to Asgard.

'You'd better tell us what you've done,' they warned a trembling Loki. 'And you had better get the apples back. Otherwise woe betide you!'

The Land of the Giants was far away and Loki had no time to lose. So he turned himself into a hawk and flew to Thiazi's castle. There he found Idunn being kept prisoner by the giant. He changed her into a hazelnut and, picking her up in his beak, he carried her away. When the giant realized what had happened, he turned back into an eagle. Furious at being tricked, he began to chase after them.

In Asgard, an enormous bonfire was lit to guide Loki safely home. By the time he saw it, the eagle was right on his tail. Loki knew that Thiazi was just about to catch him. He swooped down and the eagle followed. The heat of the bonfire singed the eagle's wings and Thiazi plunged down into the flames.

The gods were overjoyed to have Idunn and the apples back, and soon regained their strength and youthfulness. As for the god of mischief, it wasn't long before he was up to his old tricks again.

THE SAINT AND THE CHRIST CHILD

This is the story of how a man called Christopher came to be
the Christian patron saint of travellers.

Long ago, there lived a man who was said to be more than six
metres tall. Not only this, he was famous for his amazing strength.
His father worked as a blacksmith all of his life, but his son grew
up longing to be a soldier. So, as soon as he was old enough, the
boy left his home and his family to fight in the wars. But he hated the fighting
and bloodshed and soon grew tired of a soldier's life. Instead, he decided to
dedicate himself to worshipping God but did not know where to find him.
Instead, he went to live in a hut by the river and earned his living carrying
travellers across the water on his broad shoulders.

One stormy night, he heard a voice calling through the howling wind.

'Christopher, Christopher,' called the voice. 'Carry me over the river.'

When the man went outside and looked around, he thought he must be
dreaming. For the voice belonged to a very small child. He lifted the child
on to his shoulders, took his staff in his hand and stepped into the water.
The river was now a raging flood, its waters rising higher and higher.
With each stumbling step he took, the child on his back grew heavier
and heavier. Almost collapsing with exhaustion, the man cried out:

'Child, you weigh more than any burden I have ever carried.
I cannot bear your weight much longer. I shall fall.'

'Do not worry,' the child replied. 'You will not fall, for I am Jesus
Christ the Son of God, who you promised to serve. And on my
shoulders I carry the burdens of the whole world.'

And this is how the man found God and became Christopher,
a name which means the Christ-bearer. When he reached the
other side of the river, Christopher planted his staff in the
bank where it grew into a tall, straight palm tree.
Then he set out on his new life of preaching
and teaching in the service of God.

THE MONKEY KING AND THE HEAVENLY PEACHES

Many years ago, a Chinese Buddhist monk journeyed to India to learn about the life of the Buddha. He had many adventures and learned many things. This is one of the stories and legends he brought back from his travels.

Long ago, a stone monkey was born from a stone egg. The Heavenly Emperor was glad to see this brand-new creature and named it the Monkey King. The Monkey King was lively and clever. He was also ambitious. More than anything else, he wanted to be immortal and live for ever, like the gods. He pestered and pestered them to tell him how, and made their lives very miserable indeed. But they wouldn't give in. He even stole the great iron rod which governed the level of the sea. The gods were furious.

'Heaven knows what chaos he'll cause,' they muttered.

'He needs teaching a lesson and no mistake,' they said.

The monkey was much too clever to be caught. So the gods decided to play a trick on him. They invited him to a fabulous feast. 'To bury the hatchet,' they said, 'and make friends.'

The Monkey King ate so much food and drank so much wine that he couldn't move. He fell into a deep, deep sleep. While he slept, the gods carried him down to Hell and put him in a cage, guarded by ten fierce demons.

'That'll put a stop to his mischief,' chuckled the gods. 'Once and for all.'

But it didn't. Before very long, the Monkey King managed to escape. The gods had to try something different. If they made him feel important, perhaps he'd stop pestering them. So they made him Grand Master of the Heavenly Stables. But the Monkey King soon got bored. He neglected his duties and began to make trouble. And every time the gods tried to catch him and stop him, the Monkey King got away. First, he changed into a giant and strode off across the sea with giant strides. Then he turned into a fly and flew away.

It was hopeless.

Finally, the gods gave in. They put him in charge of the Heavenly Peach Garden. The Monkey King's dreams had come true. For, by stealing and eating the heavenly peaches, he too could become immortal.

But it didn't stop his terrible behaviour. He just couldn't stay out of trouble. He picked quarrels with the gods and ruined their annual peach banquet by breaking plates and spilling wine, and by spoiling all the peaches. In no time at all, the gods lost patience.

'That's it,' they said. 'Enough is enough.'

They trapped the monkey by his tail and threw him into an enormous cauldron to boil for forty-nine days and nights. Calm as you like, the Monkey King lifted the cauldron lid and peeked out.

'You'd better let me out,' he said. 'Or you'll be sorry.'

In utter despair, the gods called on the Buddha.

'Please, Lord Buddha,' they pleaded and begged. 'You must help us. We simply don't know what else to do with the wretched creature.'

The Buddha agreed. He set the Monkey King a test. If he could jump out of the Buddha's hand, he would become ruler of Heaven. The Monkey King leapt into the air with a gigantic leap and jumped right across the heavens. He wrote his name on a stone at the foot of a mighty mountain, then, with another huge bound, he leapt back again.

'There,' he boasted. 'That proves it. I've leaped across the universe and back. You can't go further than that!'

The Buddha said nothing but smiled at the monkey, a smile full of kindness and understanding. Then he pointed at his hand. The place where the stone was, at the far end of the universe, was no further than the tip of one of the Buddha's fingers!

The Monkey King had to admit defeat. There was nothing else for it. All his cleverness and boastfulness had gone. And his punishment? He was locked inside a magic mountain, until, at last, the kindly Buddha took pity on him and set him free.

THE BLESSED LAST PROPHET

For Muslims, the city of Makkah in Saudi Arabia is the holiest place in the world. This is where the Prophet Muhammad was born and where he taught people to worship Allah.

The Prophet Muhammad was born in Makkah in the year 570CE. His father, Abdullah, died before he was born. Some days before his birth, his mother, Amina, received a message from Allah telling her that her baby son would be very special. She had a dream in which she saw that a light shone from her body, bright enough to light up the whole world. Then an angel appeared before her.

'I bring you good news,' the angel said. 'Oh mother of the blessed last prophet. Your son will be the saviour of the world.'

When the baby was born, Amina named him Muhammad, which means the praised one.

As a young baby, Muhammad was cared for by his foster mother, Halima. She loved having Muhammad in her house. For while he was there, her date trees bloomed and all her sheep and camels thrived. But a terrible tragedy struck when Muhammad was six years old. His mother, Amina, fell ill and died leaving the little boy an orphan. At first, Muhammad was looked after by his grandfather and then by his uncle, Abu Talib, who loved and cared for him as if he were his own son.

When Muhammad was about 12 years old his uncle, who was a trader, announced that he had to go on a long journey to Syria. Muhammad at once wanted to go with him.

'I don't know about that,' said his uncle. 'It's a very long way and the road is dangerous. You'd be safer staying at home.'

'Please take me with you, Uncle,' pleaded Muhammad. 'I promise no harm will come to me.'

And so they set off. Next day, their caravan stopped to rest by a shady oasis near the town of Basra where a holy man, Bahira, lived in a monastery. Bahira welcomed the traders and they invited him to come and eat a meal with them.

'Stay here and guard the goods and animals,' said Abu Talib to Muhammad.

As they ate, Bahira told them of an ancient holy book that was kept in the monastery for safety. It foretold the coming of the blessed last prophet sent by Allah to save the world. The book described the tell-tale signs that would show the faithful who the prophet was. As he was talking, Bahira glanced across to where Muhammad sat guarding the animals. And what he saw amazed him. A cloud hovered above the boy's head, shading him from the hot desert sun. Not only this, the trees and stones were bowing to him, exactly as the ancient book had foretold.

In great excitement, the holy man got to his feet and raised his arms to Heaven.

'Abu Talib,' he said, 'take care of your nephew. Great things lie in store for him. He and no other is the last blessed prophet whose coming has been foretold. Do not continue your journey but take him back to Makkah and guard him with your life. For he will have many enemies wishing to see him fail.'

Then Bahira called Muhammad over to him and kissed him on the shoulder, a sign that he was indeed the blessed last prophet of Islam.

And so Muhammad and his uncle returned to Makkah. Muhammad grew up to be truthful and honest, loved and trusted by everyone. People called him 'al-Amin', which means 'the trustworthy'. He worked hard as a merchant, learning the trade from his beloved uncle who never forgot Bahira's words and continued to watch over him. When he was about 25 years old, he went to work for a wealthy widow, Khadijah. She was so impressed by Muhammad's honesty and fairness that she sent a proposal of marriage to him. Abu Tabil was delighted and blessed the match.

For many years, Muhammad was content with his life. He loved his wife and business was flourishing. But one day he began to see that the world was full of corruption and cruelty, especially towards people who were poor and unfortunate. Muhammad began to spend more and more time alone in prayer and meditation, wondering about the world he lived in and the injustices he saw. He asked himself many questions. How could people be saved? Where was the guidance they needed? For days he meditated in the peace and quiet of a solitary cave. There, on Mount Hira, he heard voices saying:

'Peace be upon you, O Messenger of God.'

But when he looked around, no one was there.

35

One night as he lay asleep, the cave was filled with a brilliant light and an angel appeared, holding a piece of cloth that was covered with writing.

'Read!' the angel told Muhammad.

'I cannot read,' Muhammad said.

'Read!' the voice repeated.

Muhammad looked again and found that he could read the words. They were as familiar as if they were written on his heart. He spoke the words aloud:

'Recite! In the name of your Lord who created, created people from drops of blood.

Recite! Your Lord is the most generous one who by the pen taught people what they did not know.'

Muhammad was terrified when he heard these words pouring out of his mouth. Where had they all come from? Wide awake now, he fled from the cave and began to run down the mountain. Then he heard the angel's voice calling after him:

'Do not be afraid,' it said. 'You are God's messenger, and I am the angel Jibril.'

Muhammad rushed home shaking and shivering, and told Khadijah what had happened. She comforted him and reassured him, for she truly believed that he was the blessed last prophet. From that day on, the angel Jibril appeared many times to Muhammad. The words he revealed, Allah's very own words, were recited by Muhammad and written down later to become the holy book, the Qur'an. And, it was at Allah's command, that Muhammad began preaching and spreading the word of Allah. He was the blessed and last prophet of Islam.

JOURNEYS THROUGH DREAMTIME

The Aborigine people of Australia believe that the landscape is sacred and was formed long ago in a time known as Dreamtime, when the spirits roamed the Earth, creating all the features of the natural world and all living things.

 There was once a wise chief called Nurunderi who was sent by the Great Spirit to shape the Earth and teach the people how to live their lives. Nurunderi travelled from north to south, creating rocks and plants and animals and dividing the hunting grounds among the people. He created all the fish in the rivers from the body of a giant cod, then placed his canoe in Heaven to become the Milky Way. He turned a tribe of people who would not listen to his teachings into birds.

When Nurunderi had completed his tasks, he began his journey back across Australia on his way home to Heaven. One day, as he walked by a lake, he heard a strange moaning coming from a tree.

'Help us! Please help us, kind stranger,' came the sound. 'We are two sisters trapped in the tree.'

Being a good man, Nurunderi took pity on them and ordered the oak tree to set them free. And when he saw how beautiful the sisters were he asked them to marry him.

Time passed by. One day, Nurunderi and his wives went fishing in the lake. While their husband paddled his canoe out into the deeper water, the two sisters cast their net in the shallows. Suddenly, one of them gave a cry.

'Look!' she said, pointing at the net. 'We've caught a huge tukkeri fish, the most delicious fish in the whole world.'

'But we're not allowed to eat it,' the other said. 'Nurunderi says it is reserved for the gods.'

The mischievous sisters looked at each other. Surely no harm would be done if they ate a tukkeri – Nurunderi need never know.

By now, Nurunderi had paddled across the lake to visit his brother-in-law.

Nobody noticed the sisters take the fish home. That evening before Nurunderi returned, they cooked the fish and ate until they could eat no more.

But as the time drew nearer for Nurunderi to come home, they began to worry about what they had done. They hid the rest of the fish so no one would find it, but they could not get rid of the smell. It was everywhere and clung to everything, no matter what they did. There was nothing else for it but to run away.

Late that night when Nurunderi reached home, the smell of tukkeri fish still hung in the air. He guessed at once what had happened.

'My wives must be punished,' he said. 'For eating the forbidden fish.'

But although he looked for them everywhere, they were nowhere to be found.

Next morning, Nurunderi took his spear and his boomerang and set off in search of his wives. He followed their footprints to the bank of the river but, once he crossed to the other side, the track was lost. For three days and three nights, he looked for his wives but never got any closer to finding them.

One night as he slept, his guardian angel, the Grandmother Spirit, whispered in his ear. 'Do not despair,' she told Nurunderi.

'Your journey is near its end.'

All next day, Nurunderi travelled on and on, until he reached the great Murray River which flows into the ocean. The Great Spirit made a bridge so that he could cross over, and on the other side he found his wives' footprints, made three days before. Not long afterwards, he discovered their campsite, with the fire still glowing and the remains of their food still warm. He wept for his wives and for what would happen to them until his tears filled a pool by the sea. And then he saw them about to walk across a causeway to an island that rose out of the ocean. Nurunderi knew that if they reached the island they would be free for ever. He prayed to the Great Spirit to tell him what to do.

'They have done wrong and must be punished,' the answer came. 'As they cross the causeway, you must sing the wind song and stir up the sea to swallow them.'

With a heavy heart, this is what Nurunderi did. As they started to cross, he sang the wind song, until the waves swelled and surged and the two sisters were drowned by the sea. Then Nurunderi turned his wives into two rocks.

It was now time for the great chief to return to Heaven. He dived into the sea and swam down and down to wash away all traces of his life on Earth. Then he rose up through the ocean and into the sky towards Heaven.

THE GREAT NIGHT JOURNEY INTO HEAVEN

After the two sacred cities of Makkah and Madinah,
the Dome of the Rock in Jerusalem is the third holiest shrine of Islam.
From here, the Prophet Muhammad made his Great Night Journey into Heaven.

 One night, the Prophet Muhammad lay asleep near the Sacred Mosque in Makkah when he was woken by the angel Jibril. The angel had come to guide him on an incredible journey. Carried on the back of a fabulous winged beast called Lightning, Muhammad sped through the dark skies to Jerusalem. There he met three of the prophets who had come to Earth before him: Ibrahim, Musa and Isa, and led them in prayer.

Then the angel Jibril brought him two jugs, one full of milk, the other of wine. Muhammad drank the milk and put the wine to one side.

'You have chosen well,' said Jibril. 'For wine is forbidden to you and all Muslims.'

Then the angel led Muhammad up a ladder of light through the seven heavens to Paradise and into the glorious presence of Allah. There, Allah spoke and gave the commandment to Muhammad that all Muslims should pray fifty times a day. On his way back down to Earth, Muhammad met Musa who asked how often Allah had commanded that Muslims should pray.

'Fifty times a day,' Muhammad replied.

'Prayer is a serious business and people are lazy,' Musa said. 'Ask your Lord to make it less. Then people will be sure to follow.'

So Muhammad returned to Allah, and ten prayers were taken off the total. Again and again, Musa objected and Muhammad returned to speak with Allah until only five prayers were left for the whole day. Muhammad could not ask Allah for any fewer than that. Instead Muhammad said:

'Whoever prays faithfully five times a day, shall have the same reward as for fifty hurried prayers.'

And this is the rule still followed by all Muslims.

Then, before dawn broke over a new day, Muhammad mounted Lightning once more and flew back through the dark skies to the sacred city of Makkah.

THE BUDDHA PASSES AWAY

For Buddhists, the most sacred places are those connected with the Buddha's life in Nepal and India: Lumbini, where he was born; Bodh Gaya, where he gained enlightenment; Sarnath, where he taught for the first time; and Kushinagara, where he passed away.

When the Buddha was about eighty years old, he knew that the time was coming for him to leave the world. He sent his faithful monks away for a well-earned rest while he spent a few days with his constant companion, Ananda. He advised Ananda:

'Do not find another leader after me. Each of you monks must be like a lamp and light your own way through life.'

Then he told Ananda to gather the monks together again in a nearby hall of worship. The Buddha reminded them of his teachings and told them to continue their hard work when he had gone. This done, he made his very last journey to the little town of Kushinagara in the far north-west of India.

On the way, a kindly blacksmith called Chunda came to see the Buddha. He invited the Buddha and his monks for a meal at his home. The blacksmith went to a great deal of effort for his honoured guests. He made sweet rice and cakes for the monks, and a special dish of mushrooms for the Buddha.

After the meal, the Buddha fell ill with terrible pains and fever. He left Chunda's house and continued his journey, stopping often to rest and for water. Just outside Kushingara, he stopped for the last time in a shady grove. Here, between two tall trees, the Buddha lay down on his right-hand side.

'Do not be sad, Ananda,' the Buddha said to his weeping companion. 'You have been my dearest friend, a king among kings. Now you must remember my teaching – everything changes and passes away. Do not grieve. Go and strive diligently.'

Then, with his monks gathered around him, the Buddha closed his eyes and passed away. And as he reached the perfect peace of nirvana, the trees about him burst into bloom and scattered their petals over his body. And the sky rained down sweet-smelling sandalwood, while the gods played their heavenly music. At last, as the monks mourned their master's death, a mighty earthquake shook the Earth to announce to all that the Buddha had passed away.

HOW THE SACRED RIVER FELL TO EARTH

This is the story of how the River Ganges, the sacred river of the Hindus, fell to Earth from its source high in Heaven to flow across India to the sea.

The gods were pleased with King Bhagiratha. He was a holy man in both word and deed, who had spent many years worshipping Shiva among the high-peaked Himalayas, the mountains where the gods lived. From far and wide, people loved and respected him. To reward the king and to show him their esteem, the gods presented him with a magnificent horse. It had been born in their own stable in Heaven and it could run like the wind on its shining hooves. The horse became King Bhagiratha's most prized possession. Then, one day, disaster struck. Jealous demons crept into the palace, stole the horse and carried it off to the underworld. King Bhagiratha was in despair and could not be consoled. He called for his sixty thousand sons.

'We will follow the demons and fetch your horse back,' they reassured their father. 'However long it might take.'

They dug and dug a great yawning chasm which stretched deep into the Earth. But they could not find a single trace of the demons and were burned to ashes by the fires of the underworld.

King Bhagiratha prayed to Lord Shiva to bring his sons back to life.

'Dear Lord Shiva,' he pleaded, 'let the river of Heaven fall from the sky and bring my sons back from the land of the dead.'

Shiva heard the prayer and took pity on the kindly king. He ordered the Ganges river to descend from Heaven, from its source in Vishnu's toe. But just as the water was about to rush downwards, a terrible thought struck the great god. If the full weight of the water crashed suddenly to Earth, the force would shatter the world. Quickly, Shiva climbed to the top of holy Mount Kailasa and sat on the snow-capped summit. And as the river fell, he caught it in his long, matted hair. The Ganges flowed through his hair for many years, then Shiva let it trickle very slowly and fall at last in a cascading stream to the mountains below.

Now, as the river flowed down to Earth, it flooded the home of
a holy man, Jahnu, who was so angry that he drank all its waters in
a single gulp. King Bhagiratha began to despair of ever seeing his
sons again.

'I beg you, good Jahnu,' the king asked the holy man, 'to give the
river back. Only then can I bring my sons back to life.'

Jahnu took pity on the king and released the river, which flowed
out from his ear. Then King Bhagiratha led the water away from
the mountains, across the plains and over the sea, until he
reached the underworld and the land of the dead.

There, the sacred waters of the Ganges washed
over his dead sons' ashes, and all sixty thousand
came back to life. And that is how the great
river of Heaven first fell down to Earth.

DAY TIME, NIGHT TIME

In Africa, people believed that the world and everything in it were created by
a great and powerful spirit with a little help from the animals...

 When the world was first made, it was never cold and darkness never
fell. The warm Sun shone and lit up the world by day and the bright
Moon shone and lit up the world by night. Then one day, God called
Bat to him and gave him a basket to take to the Moon. The basket was
full of black darkness and was closed shut with a tight-fitting lid.

'On no account must you open the basket,' God warned Bat. 'Tell the Moon I will
follow and explain what to do.'

Bat flew off carrying the basket on his back. It was a long and tiring flight to the
Moon. After a while, he felt exhausted and hungry
and stopped to look for something to
eat. He put the basket down on the
ground by the side of the road. While
Bat was off hunting, some animals
trotted down the road and discovered
the basket lying there. Hoping that it
was full of food, they pulled off its lid
and peeked inside.

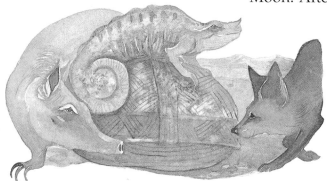

'Stop!' shouted Bat, swooping towards them. 'Whatever you do, please don't
open the basket!'

But his warning came too late. Even before he had finished speaking, the
darkness had all escaped and filled the sky. The only light came from the Moon,
shining like a lamp in the blackness. And this is how
day and night came to be.

From that time to this, Bat sleeps all
day. But when dusk falls he flies to and
fro, hither and thither, trying to capture
the darkness again. If only he can put it
back in the basket, he can obey God's
wishes to take it to the Moon. But Bat
never quite succeeds in his task for day
always breaks too soon.

THE CLEVER HUNTER AND THE MOON SPIRIT

This ancient story is told in Malaysia to explain
how humans first learned right from wrong.

 In the beginning, people had no laws or rules. They lied and cheated, and behaved very badly. The rules of good behaviour existed, but they were secrets kept by a wicked spirit who lived in the Moon. His name was Moyang Melur and he was half-man, half-tiger. Now Moyang Melur did not like to share his secrets, so he kept the rules all to himself.

One night, the noise and chaos coming from the Earth was so great that it woke him up. He leaned out of the Moon for a better look, but as he looked, he leaned too far and plunged to the ground. Luckily, he landed unhurt. Then he met a hunter, called Moyang Kapir.

'If you don't help me get back to the Moon at once,' he snarled at the hunter, in his loudest, most threatening voice. 'I'll kill you and everyone else on the Earth!'

Moyang Kapir threw a rope up to the Moon and the two climbed up together. Now, the wicked spirit had worked out a cunning plan. As soon as they reached the Moon, he would kill the hunter and eat him. But Moyang Kapir was too quick and clever to be caught and he escaped down the rope back to Earth. In his hand he carried the bag of secrets, which contained the rules of behaviour that the spirit had kept hidden under a mat.

So, Moyang Kapir shared out the rules among the people to teach them how to behave and to live together in harmony.

THE BRAVE HARE AND THE BUDDHA

A collection of tales called the Jatakas tell of the Buddha's past lives. In many of these he appears as an animal to teach a particular lesson. In this story, the Buddha disguises himself as a hare to show the importance of making sacrifices.

A hare once lived in a beautiful forest near a stream as blue as the sea. The grass all around was soft and green, and the trees full of flowers and fruit. Now, though the hare was big and strong, he was also wise and the other animals looked up to him as their king. Three of them – a monkey, a jackal and an otter – became his special friends. Every evening they would meet and talk about many things. Under the hare's good influence they became kind and caring to the other creatures, and gave up their bad ways.

One evening as they all sat together, the hare looked up at the Moon. It was shining and full in the dark night sky.

'Tomorrow will be a holy day,' he said. 'We should try to do something to mark it. Let's go without eating for the day, and give our food away to anyone who asks for it.'

The others agreed.

Next morning, the monkey went to the mountain and gathered some juicy ripe mangoes. He took them home, put them aside and waited for someone to come.

'If nobody comes, I'll have a fine feast tomorrow,' he thought. Meanwhile, the jackal found a dead lizard and a jug of milk lying outside a hut. Nobody claimed them when he asked. So he took them home and wondered if anyone would want them.

'If not, I'll have a fine feast tomorrow,' he thought.

The otter found some fish by the river, left there by a fisherman. Nobody claimed them so he took them home and waited, dreaming of tomorrow's fine feast.

The hare set off to find some food, but then he had a terrible thought. All he usually ate was grass. Surely no one would ask for that? The only other thing he had to offer in the world was himself. And so this is what he vowed to do.

Sakka, Lord of Heaven, heard the hare's vow and decided to test it out. At lunchtime, disguised as a poor traveller, he set off for the forest.

'Oh woe, oh woe what am I to do?' he wailed. 'I've lost all my money and food. Can anyone give me something to eat?'

The monkey appeared with his juicy mangoes. But the traveller refused to take them. Neither did he want the jackal's lizard and milk, nor the otter's fish. Then he saw the hare.

'You can eat me if you like,' squeaked the hare, bravely.

'Thank you, kind hare,' said Sakka. 'I will.'

Then Sakka conjured up a fine, glowing fire with leaping, golden flames. And the hare rushed towards it and leapt straight into the middle. But the flames did not feel hot to him at all. They were cool and refreshing like rain. Then Sakka took the hare in his soft, jewelled hands and lifted him up into Heaven. He told the gods of the hare's great courage and of the sacrifice he had been willing to make.

Then, to remember his deeds for ever and ever, he drew the shape of the hare on the face of the Moon, where it can still be seen to this day.

THE EXODUS FROM EGYPT

The three most important festivals in the Jewish year are Pesach, Shavuot and Sukkot.
They are called the three pilgrim festivals. They celebrate the Israelites' (Jews') escape
from slavery in Egypt, the giving of the Ten Commandments to Moses by God,
and the arrival of the Jews in the Promised Land. This is the story of
the Exodus from Egypt and of the Ten Commandments.

When Moses led the Israelites out of slavery in Egypt, they had been
living there for more than four hundred years. Now they were forced
to flee through the desert on their long, long journey to the Promised
Land. They travelled both by night and by day, so keen were they to
get far away from Egypt. By day, God went in front of them in a pillar of cloud to
show them the way and, by night, in a pillar of fire.

When the Pharaoh heard of the Israelites' departure, he was furious.

'Who will be our servants now?' he raged. 'We must find the
Israelites and fetch them back.'

So he set off in pursuit, and took his army with him, riding in
six hundred of his finest war chariots. He found the Israelites
camped near the Red Sea. The Israelites were terrified at the
awesome sight of the Egyptian army galloping towards them.
They called to Moses, their leader.

'Why have you brought us here to die?' they cried.
'We would have been better off in Egypt.'

'Don't be afraid,' Moses replied. 'If you trust in God, he will
save you. Be calm and follow me.'

The Israelites looked around. In front of them stood the Egyptian army, ready to attack. Behind them lay the sea. In either direction their path was blocked.

Then God spoke to Moses:

'Lift up your staff and stretch out your hand over the sea to divide the waters,' he said. 'Then lead the Israelites over the dry sea floor.'

Moses did as God commanded. He stretched out his hand over the sea and lifted up his staff. All that night, a strong wind blew and pushed back the waters of the sea. By morning, it had been split in two with a pathway of dry land running through the middle. Then the Israelites followed Moses onto the path, walking with high walls of water to their left and right.

'After them!' shouted the Pharaoh. And the Egyptians raced after them into the sea with all their horses, chariots and riders. But the wheels of their chariots stuck in the sand and the horses's hooves sank into the mud of the sea bed. They could not catch the Israelites.

When the Israelites were safely across, God spoke again to Moses:

'Stretch out your hand over the sea, so its waters flow back together again and cover the Egyptians, their horses and chariots.'

And Moses did as God commanded. As the thundering waters closed around them, the Egyptians tried to flee, but all of them were drowned. God had saved the Israelites.

For many long years after that, the Israelites wandered through the wilderness on their way to Canaan, the Promised Land. They faced many trials and many tough times and often despaired of reaching their goal. But God always looked after them, sending bread from Heaven for them to eat and guiding them on their way.

Some months after their escape from Egypt, the Israelites reached Mount Sinai. All around was dusty desert and this is where they pitched their tents. Then Moses went up the mountain to pray. Here, God spoke to him again.

'Ask the Israelites if they are ready to follow me and be my chosen people,' God said.

'If they say yes, I shall appear to you in three days' time, and reveal my laws to you.'

Three days later, the Israelites stood at the foot of the mountain waiting patiently for God to appear. The top of the mountain was circled in cloud, thunder boomed and flashes of lightning lit up the sky.

Then, the sound of a trumpet split the air, sounding loud and clear. Trembling with fear, the Israelites called on Moses to save them. The trumpet sounded louder and louder and fire licked the sides of the mountain. Then God called Moses to the mountain:

'These are my laws for you and your people,' he said. And the laws were these:

'I am the Lord your God. You must worship no other gods but me.

Do not worship idols (statues).

You shall not take my name in vain.

Remember to keep the Sabbath holy. For that is the day on which your God rested after he created the world.

Respect your father and mother.

Do not kill.

Do not commit adultery.

Do not steal.

Do not wrongly accuse others.

Do not be envious of other people or of their homes or possessions.

These are my commandments for you.'

When Moses came down from the mountain, he told the people what God had said.

'We will do everything that God commands,' they replied.

Then Moses wrote the Ten Commandments on two great slabs of stone and after many more years wandering the wilderness, the Israelites carried the Commandments out of the desert and into the Promised Land.

THE HUNGRY GHOSTS

At the Buddhist Festival of Hungry Ghosts in China and Japan, the story is told of the monk, Mu-lien, who tried to save his mother from Hell.

 There once lived a pious man called Mu-lien who became one of the Buddha's chief disciples. One day, Mu-lien had to leave home on a long journey, far, far away. Before he left, he gave his mother a large sum of money to give away to the monks who came to her door. But his greedy mother kept the money for herself and lied to Mu-lien when he returned, pretending that she had given it all away. Because of her lie, Mu-lien's mother went to Hell when she died – to suffer forever in anguish and torment.

Now Mu-lien was not only pious, he was also kind and wise and he decided to try to save his mother. So he set off for Hell to find her. On his way he met Yama, the King of Hell.

'Your mother lied and must be punished,' Yama told Mu-lien, sternly. 'You can't save her. No one can.'

And then he stomped away.

But brave Mu-lien would not be put off. He visited the judges who had sentenced his mother in King Yama's court.

'A very serious case indeed,' they muttered and shook their heads sadly. 'We had no choice but to send her to the deepest part of Hell. That should teach her a lesson.'

Mu-lien continued his journey down and down into the deepest, darkest part of Hell. It was not a place for the frightened or faint-hearted. Almost at once, Mu-lien was attacked by a gang of fifty bull-headed monsters, each with a mouth full of ferocious fangs as sharp as swords, voices like thunder, and eyes which flashed lightning and flames.

But Mu-lien carried a magic wand, a gift from the Buddha himself. He waved it and at once the hideous monsters disappeared.

Finally, he reached the lowest parts of Hell and the jailer showed him to his mother's cell. Mu-lien's eyes filled with tears to see his mother in such a pitiful state. She was tied to a bed by forty-nine long chains, each so strong it would take a hundred men to break it. The only person with the power to release her and to forgive her for her sins, was the Lord Buddha himself.

In great despair, Mu-lien went straight to the Buddha.

'I beg you, Lord Buddha,' pleaded Mu-lien. 'Please release my mother. I will make sure that in her next life on Earth she devotes herself to doing good works.'

'Very well, Mu-lien,' the Buddha replied. 'You are a good and holy man, and I will help you. But there is one condition I must impose. Every year, at this time, your mother must offer a feast to the Buddha and all the monks, to make amends for her meanness. Then, and only then, can she go free.'

And so every year, on the day of the Festival of Hungry Ghosts, Mu-lien's mother cooked the Buddha and his monks a sumptuous feast. And she always saved some food for the hungry ghosts, still imprisoned in Hell, without a peaceful place to rest. Because she knew how terrible that could be.

THE FIVE BELOVED ONES

The festival of Baisakhi is a very important time for Sikhs. It is held in April and marks the start of the Sikh new year. It is also the day on which the Khalsa, a close-knit band of devout Sikhs, was formed in 1699. This is the story of that day.

 On Baisakhi Day, in 1699, the last great Sikh teacher, Guru Gobind Singh, summoned all the Sikhs to the town of Anandpur. For many years, the Sikhs had struggled to defend their faith against the rulers of India who tried to stop the Sikhs from worshipping. Guru Gobind Singh wanted the Sikhs to be brave, strong and ready to fight hard for their beliefs, even if it meant fighting to the death. He now stood before the huge crowd of Sikhs dressed in uniform, his sword gleaming in his hand.

'Is there anyone ready to die for their faith?' he asked them. 'Who will give me their head?'

Everyone fell silent. Nobody moved and nobody answered the Guru's question. Why was he trying to frighten them? Had he gone mad to ask such a thing?

Then the Guru repeated his question.

'Is there anyone ready to die for their faith?' he asked. 'Step forward and offer your head.'

Still nobody moved. A third time the Guru asked the same question. And this time a man came forward.

'You can take my head,' he said. 'I will die for my faith.'

Guru Gobind Singh led the man into his tent. A few minutes later, the crowd heard a loud thud. Then Guru Gobind Singh came out of his tent, holding his sword which was dripping with blood. He asked for another volunteer and another man stepped forward.

'You can take my head,' he said. 'I will die for my faith.'

Once again, the Guru led him into his tent. And as before, when he came out his sword was dripping with blood.

Twice more, Guru Gobind Singh repeated his demand. And twice more, the same thing happened. He led each brave man into his tent and reappeared with his blood-stained sword. The people in the crowd watched in silent fear, or left Anandpur altogether. They simply did not know what to do or think.

After the fifth man had entered the Guru's tent, a gasp went up from the crowd. For this time, when the Guru came out again, he brought out all five men with him.

And they were all unhurt and alive. All were dressed just like the Guru, in saffron uniforms tied with blue sashes and saffron turbans. Each one of them carried a long, curved sword in his hands. The Guru named them 'the Panj Piares', which means 'the five beloved ones'.

'You have passed the test I set with flying colours,' he told them. 'And shown you are not afraid to die. Now, my brothers, you are the same as me. For you have been chosen by God as my five beloved ones.'

Then the Guru turned to the crowd, whose feelings had changed to surprise.

'Do not be frightened,' the Guru told them. 'These men have showed that they are willing to fight to defend our beliefs. They are the pure ones who were willing to die. They are the first members of the Khalsa, ready to spread our Sikh faith far and wide. Any of you can join the Khalsa, women as well as men.'

Then a great ceremony was held to welcome the five men into the holy order, with many others from the crowd. First they drank the sweet water of life, or amrit, from a steel bowl. Then they made a solemn vow to wear their uniform at all times and to live according to the gurus' teachings. The Guru reminded them that all members of the Khalsa were equal in God's eyes and in his own. To show this, they would all have equal names. So all the men were called Singh, meaning lion, and all the women Kaur, meaning princess.

Ever since then, at every Baisakhi and on many other days besides, the amrit ceremony takes place in the gurdwara (temple) and people are welcomed into the Khalsa. And five devout Sikhs are chosen to play the parts of the first Panj Piares who joined the Guru almost three hundred years ago.

THE GOOD PRINCE AND THE WICKED WITCH

This is the story of Holi, the great Hindu festival of spring
which is celebrated each year in February or March.

 There was once an evil demon king called Hiranyakashipu, whose name means 'golden-robed'. He was loud and boastful, cruel and arrogant and he made his courtiers' lives a misery. They waited on him hand and foot, with never a single word of thanks. The excuse for this dreadful behaviour was that wicked King Hiranyakashipu thought he was God. He made everyone obey his commands and agree with whatever he said. And woe betide anyone who did not bow down and worship him as soon as he entered the room. In fact, he acted as if he owned the world.

Now, King Hiranyakashipu had a son called Prahlad, who was gentle and kind and loved by all. But like everyone else in the palace, Prahlad grew up thinking his father was God. One day, Prahlad was in the village playing by the potter's workshop when he heard the potter praying.

'What are you doing?' Prahlad asked.

'I'm praying to Lord Vishnu, who is God, to save the lives of my poor kittens,' the potter said. 'They fell into a pot and got put in the kiln by mistake.'

'But why aren't you praying to my father?' said Prahlad.

'Why should I?' the potter said, in surprise. 'Your father isn't God.'

Prahlad secretly thought that the potter was being very foolish. If his words ever reached the King's ears, the potter would surely be killed. But when he watched the potter take the pot out of the kiln, Prahlad changed his mind. For out of the pot climbed four squeaking kittens, who seemed none the worse for their ordeal. The delighted potter gave thanks to Lord Vishnu. From that day, Prahlad no longer believed his father was God but worshipped Lord Vishnu instead.

Then one day, his father asked Prahlad who he thought was the greatest being in the whole wide world.

'You are the King,' replied Prahlad, at once. 'But God is far greater than you.'

The King was so furious, he spluttered with rage.

'Take this vile child away!' he shrieked at his soldiers. 'And throw him into a pit full of poisonous snakes.'

The soldiers did as they were told. But none of the snakes would bite Prahlad, for Lord Vishnu was watching over him. Instead, they coiled around him and let him stroke their heads until the soldiers pulled him out of the pit.

The King was livid. He was determined to kill his son. That evening, when Prahlad was fast asleep, the King sent the royal elephants to trample him to death. But Lord Vishnu again protected him and Prahlad did not even wake up. All he remembered was having a strange dream.

Next, the King ordered his soldiers to charge at Prahlad and kill him with their swords. They obeyed the command, but still could not hurt him.

'You're a very lucky little boy,' his father fumed.

'It wasn't luck,' brave Prahlad replied. 'It was God who saved me.'

At this, King Hiranyakashipu almost exploded with rage.

'We'll see about that,' he screamed.

In a terrible temper, the King went to see his sister the wicked witch, Holika, to ask for her advice.

'Whatever shall I do?' he wailed. 'If you can't help me, nobody can.'

'I've got a plan,' Holika cackled, 'to get rid of Prahlad once and for all. We'll build a huge bonfire and I'll carry him into it. That way he can't escape. For my magic powers mean that I cannot be hurt by fire. So I will be safe, and Prahlad will be dead! Hee! hee! hee!'

And this is what they did. Next day, the King ordered a massive bonfire to be lit and Holika carried Prahlad into the middle. She sat down calmly, as the flames licked over them.

'It's just a game,' she told him with a sneer.

But Lord Vishnu was watching over Prahlad as he had done so many times before. He took away Holika's magic powers and granted them to the child instead. So Prahlad was unharmed by the fire while his wicked aunt perished in the flames. When the King saw this, he was forced to admit defeat and to accept that Lord Vishnu was truly God.

And people still light a bonfire on the first day of Holi, to remember the story of little Prince Prahlad and Holika, the wicked witch, and of how good overcame evil. To celebrate, they throw on coconuts to roast as offerings to the gods. And when the coconuts are cool, they eat them!

GLOSSARY

Allah The Muslim name for God.

angel In Christianity and Islam, a messenger of God.

avatars The forms or shapes taken by the Hindu god, Vishnu, when he visits the Earth to save it from danger. The most famous avatars are the gods, Rama and Krishna.

Baisakhi An important Sikh festival which marks the Sikh New Year and the formation of the first Khalsa (community, or family, of Sikhs) in 1699.

BCE Initials for 'Before Common Era'. They are used to write dates before the year 0, which is when Jesus Christ is said to have been born. BC (Before Christ) is also used.

Bible The Christian holy book, divided into the Old Testament (containing Jewish writings) and the New Testament (containing the story of Jesus and his teachings).

Buddha A great teacher who lived in India in the 6th century BCE. Followers of the Buddhist faith use his teachings as their guide through life.

Buddhism An ancient faith based on the teachings of the Buddha. Buddhism began in India but has since spread to many parts of South East Asia, Japan and China.

CE Initials for 'Common Era', used to write dates after the year 0. AD (Anno Domini) is also used.

Christianity A religion which began in the 1st century CE in the Middle East. Its followers, called Christians, follow the teachings of Jesus Christ who they believe to be the son of God.

Dreamtime A time, thousands of years ago, when the Aborigines (the original people of Australia) believe that their ancestors roamed across Australia, creating the landscape and all living things.

Guru Gobind Singh The tenth and last of the Sikh Gurus (teachers). He began the Khalsa.

Hinduism A very ancient religion which began in India some 4,500 years ago. Today, it has about 700 million followers, called Hindus.

Islam A religion which began in Makkah, Saudi Arabia, in the 6th century CE. Muslims believe in one God (Allah) who revealed his wishes for the world to the prophet Muhammad.

Jainism An ancient religion which began in western India in the 6th century BCE. It was founded by a holy man called Mahavira.

Jatakas A collection of stories which tell of the Buddha's past lives in which he often appeared as an animal to teach a lesson.

Jerusalem A city in Israel which is special for Jews, Christians and Muslims.

Jesus Christ The founder of Christianity, who was born a Jew about 2,000 years ago in the Middle East.

Jews Followers of the Jewish religion (Judaism) which began in the Middle East some 4,000 years ago. Also called Israelites.

Mahavira A holy man and teacher who founded the Jain religion in India in the 6th century BCE. His name is a title which means 'great hero'. He was the last of 24 teachers believed to have visited the Earth in times of crisis.

Makkah The city in Saudi Arabia where the Prophet Muhammad was born and first taught people about Allah. It is the Muslims' holiest city. It is also written as Mecca.

Moses A great Jewish leader who lived about 3,500 years ago. God chose Moses to lead the Jews out of Egypt and to receive the Ten Commandments.

Muhammad The last and greatest prophet of Islam. He was chosen by Allah to teach people how Allah wished them to live. He was born in Makkah in 570CE.

Muslim A person who follows the religion of Islam.

Myth A story, or legend, that explains a difficult idea such as good and evil.

Pesach One of the most important Jewish festivals. It celebrates the Exodus (escape) of the Jews from Egypt where they had lived miserable lives as slaves.

prophet A person chosen by God to tell people about his wishes for the world.

religion A set of beliefs and a way of worship often based on the teachings of a holy person.

Qur'an The Muslim holy book.

Shinto The ancient religion of Japan. Its followers worship spirits, called kami, which live in mountains, trees and other natural places. The most important kami is Amaterasu, the Sun goddess.

Sikhism A religion which began in India about 500 years ago. Its followers are called Sikhs.

Ten Commandments The ten most important rules for Jews and Christians to follow.

Vikings or Norsemen, were sea-farers and warriors from Scandinavia who conquered many parts of Europe from the 8th–11th centuries CE. They had many myths and legends.

INDEX